To:

....

From:

....

West Side Publishing is a division of Publications International, Ltd.

Louis Weber, CEO
Publications International, Ltd.
7373 North Cicero Avenue
Lincolnwood, Illinois 60712

ISBN-13: 978-1-4127-1583-6
ISBN-10: 1-4127-1583-0

Manufactured in China.

8 7 6 5 4 3 2 1

Kids Say the Cutest Things About
Moms

Illustrations by Amanda Haley

WEST
SIDE
PUBLISHING

Don't ever try to rub off a kiss from your Mom. That just makes it stick harder.

Alex, age 9

My Mom makes the best peanut butter sandwiches. What does she do to them?

Shane, age 7

Before I cross the street,
I look both ways and my Mom
looks all the other ways.

India, age 7

My Mom makes me laugh
when she dusts my Dad
while he watches TV.

Freddy, age 9

Mom, weren't there colors
when you were born?

Scott, age 5

I help *my Mom* at the grocery store by reaching the too-low things.

Max, age 6

My Mom never gets tired,
except in the night when I
need water.

Jill, age 6

When *my* Mom drives carpool, she's the boss of the radio.

Reese, age 10

Santa uses the same
wrapping paper my
Mom uses!

Jordon, age 6

When I feel sick, my Mom gets
to have a stay-home day.

Stella, age 6

When my Mom helps in my classroom, she gives me a secret wink.

Demitri, age 9

My Mom says some words a lot, like, "Because I said so."

Jacque, age 10

My Mom worries about me
so I don't have to.

Wyatt, age 8

If I pick out my own
clothes, my Mom says,
"Oh my," and then she smiles.

Riley, age 8

My Mom does yummy stuff with hamburger meat. She's sort of magic like that.

Douglas, age 7

Moms cry when you start school, but then they make you go back.

Alex, age 6

My Mom makes me laugh when she rides the roller coaster with me!

Kara, age 10

My Mom always knows when
I forget to wash my hands.

Marcel, age 10

Sometimes we're so loud, our Mom can't think straight!

Gwen, age 10

Everything I need is in my
Mom's purse.

Jenny, age 9

When I help my Mom bake cupcakes, she doesn't care if we make a mess.

Leah, age 9

My Mom's not very good
at playing hide-and-seek.
I always find her!

Iliana, age 6

My Mom wakes me up by yelling, "We're late!"

Ben, age 11

I like to kiss my Mom,
except for when she smells
like coffee or onions.

Maddy, age 7

Moms are good at helping kids, even when we're practically grown up.

Ari, age 8

I get embarrassed when
my Mom sticks love notes in
my lunch bag.

Kemo, age 11

My Mom says she doesn't
need her alarm clock
because me and my brother
wake her up just fine.

Kendra, age 9

My favorite time with my Mom is when we go to the diner and eat bread and butter and talk.

Glenn, age 9

My Mom does her job work
in the day and her family
work at night.

Janie, age 9

My Mom fixes me a snack to make my homework easier.

James, age 10

Moms show love with kisses
and hugs, and they even
bake brownies when they
have time.

Maria, age 9

When my Mom was my age,
CDs were a lot bigger!

Noah, age 8

My Mom likes me to keep my room clean, but she does it so much better.

Aiden, age 10

Some Moms sit on a bench at the park, but *my* Mom goes on the tire swing with *me*.

Lola, age 7

My Mom plays catch with me, but she won't throw very hard.

Jake, age 8

My Mom can read bedtime stories with her eyes closed!

Shelby, age 7

Amanda Haley graduated from The School of the Art Institute of Chicago with a BFA in painting and drawing. She has illustrated more than 40 children's books, including both fictional and educational titles. Haley lives in Virginia with her husband, Brian, and dog, Mayzie.

Publications International, Ltd., wishes to thank the following schools for their submissions to *Kids Say the Cutest Things About Moms*:
Brennermann School (Chicago, IL), Bush Elementary School (Fulton, MO), Conn-West Elementary School (Grandview, MO), Gilkey Elementary School (Plainwell, MI), Holy Family School (Granite City, IL), Kennedy Middle School (Kankakee, IL), King Lab Magnet School (Evanston, IL), Plantation Park Elementary School (Plantation, FL), St. Agatha Catholic Academy (Chicago, IL), Starr Elementary School (Plainwell, MI)